THE PORTAGE POETRY
SERIES

Series Titles

The Almost-Children
Cassondra Windwalker

Meditations of a Beast
Kristine Ong Muslim

Praise for
Cassondra Windwalker

"With taut, beautiful, and oft-haunting prose, Cassondra Windwalker gives us a book of unforgettable poetry that burrows into your heart and mind in equal measure."
—Seven Jane, author of *The Isle of Gold*

"Sad poems for sad times. Windwalker brings her lyrical style to these empathetic poems reminiscent of Rollo May's *The Courage to Create*."
—Jason Dias, author of *Finding Life on Mars*

"*The Almost-Children* is a flat-out amazing collection. Poems such as "new definitions" and "after the accident" are especially moving when each line is slowly pulled from the page and examined. It's then that the reader becomes aware of how Windwalker frames these quieter, more intimate moments through deft word choice and subtle flourishes."
—Alcy Leyva, author of *And Then There Were Crows*

"*The Almost-Children* is filled with raw emotion, eloquently expressed through Ms. Windwalker's poetic style. The images evoked by these poems will stay with me for years to come."
—Lanie Goodell, author of *Salvagium*

"Windwalker has captured that sadness which confronts us at unexpected moments after the death of a loved one."
—Virginia Walters, *Peninsula Clarion*

the
almost-children

Poems by
Cassondra Windwalker

Cornerstone Press
Stevens Point, Wisconsin

Cornerstone Press, Stevens Point, Wisconsin 54481
Copyright © 2019 Cassondra Windwalker
www.uwsp.edu/cornerstone

Printed in the United States of America.

Library of Congress Control Number: 2019934863
ISBN: 978-0-9668488-8-5

Gratefully acknowledged are the following publications:

"The Empty Bowl" first appeared in *DoveTales*.
"I Buried My Sparrow" first appeared on *The Poet's Billow*.

Cornerstone Press titles are produced in courses and internships offered by the Department of English at the University of Wisconsin–Stevens Point.

DIRECTOR & PUBLISHER-IN-CHIEF
Dr. Ross K. Tangedal

EXECUTIVE EDITOR
Jeff Snowbarger

DEVELOPMENT COORDINATOR
Alexis Neeley

SENIOR PRESS ASSISTANTS
Emmalea Stirn
Madeline Krueger

SPRING 2019 STAFF
Madeline Swanger, Katy Nachampassak, Monica Swinick, Jeremy Wolfe, Caleb Baeten, Ashley Nickel, Michaela Bargender, Grace Tesch, Elizabeth Strobel, Elizabeth Olson, Rachel Zach, Jacoby Schroeder, Breanna Camalieri, Angela Stoker, Chris Dax, Brendan Gallert, Emma Hogenson, Claire McMannes, Madeline Sibilsky, Eve Kramer

To all the almosts,
those we have lost, and those we might have become

Also by Cassondra Windwalker

Bury the Lead

Parable of Pronouns

Poems

The Almost-Children

I have begun to keep an orphanage.

It started innocently enough:
a plate of food for the hungry,
a moment of peace for the shared confidence,
an embrace for the aching –
but too soon I found these ghosts
could not be shaken, I could not keep
their forms in safe and quiet cages,
I could not still the feet that ran
to keep up with my own.

How cruel would that be, after all,
to think of banishing from my pages
and from my recollection those who have been
banished
already from the earth?
So I keep an orphanage and play mother
to these almost-children, the would-have-beens,
and cannot-give-ups who dog my steps
and look out on life only through my eyes,

and I wonder, which of us
is keeping alive the other?

the became

even the dullest pebble glows
gem-like in the prism of river and sun

oil spills become rainbows

sea-swamped eyes see mermaids
where sea-lions bask in the gloaming

a coward becomes an objector

an ink-stained envelope with ragged edges
stands effigy to a love letter
as long as it remains unread

as long as I don't ask,
you might still have answered me

its spectacular flight rendered stained glass
by my tears, the hummingbird becomes more
than bird, becomes farewell
more spirit than feathers, more wish than pres-
ence

I am untumbled, unlit, unlifted
still bound to my bones
and caught unbecoming.

Pleadings of a Drunk

Why must you follow me, sweet?
I know the measure of a cup.
I am content with the grain
that fills my palm: but you
press on me grapes and olives,
and against my will, I find myself
drunk on your presence once again:

a true daughter of spirits,
the only hangover I've ever known
is yours, Joy, and it's a beast:
the inescapable tragedy that trails
in your steps, dejected but undeterred,
a poor fever, perhaps, but a certain one –

leave me in peace, sweet.
I need no wild transports.
I can endure no more descents.

present-tense

no longer alive.

from this moment on,
everything will be defined
by what it is not,
by what is absent,
by what it cannot become.

coffee that isn't drunk,
dirty clothes that aren't picked up,
that thing you reminded yourself
to tell me, hours before
you were undone,
we were undone:

bruises that won't color
blood that won't spill.
you aren't, we aren't,
and now I don't know
what I am.

where light stops

here the zenith of the sun barely strikes
the tops of the spruce trees,
a slivered crescent of day that begins
and ends in the same sky
and leaves the wolf of darkness ever crouched
at my back, content in his unthreatened repose
to merely stretch and growl from time to time,
till the last drops of day are spilled out
across the earth, and he will rise, unhurried,
to his long prowl: I watch that traveling sunlight
as it presses through the trees
to fall in long, glittering, golden fingers
against the snow, and I think of all the light
still caught, trapped against the other side
of those dark limbs and bunching needles.
I think of all the light that cannot reach me.

the missing

Magic winks out too, it turns out:
a foggy sea, frothing ice, churns
its wrath up, up, up, the shore
and seems to promise, one day,
to swallow bluff and cliff as it swallows sand:

remnants of the surf lie abandoned
on the glistening onyx of a volcanic beach,
and amidst the shattered shells and scattered rocks,
impossible colors cast their tiny lights:
so easily missed and so suddenly quenched –

how can these strange creatures,
who braved the icy tide and the brutal glower
of winter, so suddenly wink out
here on the black sand? I try
to catch them, to mark their edges,
to count their colors: fuchsia, violet,
magenta, teal, colors that mock the austere
and defy the grim: whose children were these?

Where have they gone?
My fingers pass through them:
I cannot catch them, cannot keep them here.
Where have they gone?

we must go on

my rag-tag band hangs close –
they know that other, colder eyes
would banish them from my company,
would find our little league unhealthy
in its persistence, but I find hope
free of the odors of blood and oil too fanciful
for consolation: I will take fellowship
here among my almost-children,
and in their substantiation, attested
by my eyes and proven by my spirit,
take courage for the constancy of my own.

traveling with spectres

Almost unconsciously, I shift, making room
for them in elevators and grocery-store lines,
reaching back for immaterial hands as I cross
the street or make passage through some crowd:
I turn up the radio so I can hear the lyrics
over the constant murmur of their voices,
and when captured in the silence of some great vista,
I look back, making sure they haven't missed it.

At night, I must tuck them in
one by one, my mind intent on the pretense
that I can keep these phantoms safer
than I could protect their shattered shells,
finding solace in sleep only when I am certain
of their counterfeit peace:
they do not haunt my dreams
they have no need for concourse there,
for I have knitted them too securely
into my waking hours for them to ever fear the sun.

I wonder that you do not see them,
do not perceive how their silhouettes alter
the shape of us, but then,
I do not think they see you either.
These children are entirely my own.

Abigail

At Petroglyph Cliffs

Stories in stone draw us into the desert,
compel us to chance the cliffs and crevasses,
to fix our feet on a path pounded out
by other beings we cannot bear to divorce
from ourselves – their language is strange and harsh,
falling on our ears in a melody we cannot match,
their leathered skin wrinkling and folding
over eyes whose vantage we cannot share,
their hands full of treasures we cannot count,
but still – they tell stories. The shape of their words
is unfamiliar, but the music and the ripple
that they make when they strike the surface
of our thoughts create a resonance that we know,
reverberates through the thousand years
of our divide and makes eager children of us all:

Light the fire, then, and sit cross-legged
in the dust. Dangle brave fingers
over the abyss and laugh in terror as the wind
snatches at your hand and whispers in your ear
its false promises to carry you to the next ridge.

Take a stick, a song, a chisel,
and leave your mark – this fierce country,
with its mysteries and its lies, makes storytellers
of us all, and while we make our trade in words,
no weapon nor time can hope to estrange us.

Where We Meet

Discordance is the mortal lullaby,
this reassurance that we are more and less
than the stuff of which we are made,
than the stuff to which we are reduced:

I took the softest fabric I could find
and counted out golden stitches with my needle
I strung tiny, glass-like shells on a leather cord,
I pounded letters and leaves onto a strip
of calfskin, I clutched an eagle feather –
already pinched and shorn of its memory
of the river winds – I took all the baby's finery

and I laid it in the dust. With sweating hands
that shook in the heat and the heights,
I piled rock after rock beneath the witness
of the cliff and fixed my eyes on the promise
of the ravine, of the canyon, of the open air:
her bones, her hair, her flesh are not here,
but I give name and voice to her spirit,
I give place to footsteps that follow my own
back along the canyon paths –

more than skin and something less than divine,
she barely had time to be carnal,
so I will build this carnal cairn for her,
will anchor her shiftless spirit to its strange origin
of dust and blood and decay till she tugs
me free of my own ropes and coils,
till that melody fades, and I find a new song beyond
the stars.

not too late

it is late to say your name –
a year since you left
without ever having drawn a single breath.

the only mark you left then
was blood, but now the beating
of your heart has become the battery
of the wind, the percussion of the rain
that strikes my skin, and I cannot
own you wholly gone

I will tether you to this place you quit
with a name, with your name.
I will cast this fetter however far
I must to draw you back
just long enough to tell you this:

you did not die an unnamed thing.
then I will tell you one thing more:
Good-bye, my Abigail.

a ravenous bite

They fill my palm – tiny cool bits
of blood and bone on which I once counted
the marvels of life – your mother's baby teeth.
Sharp little things that pierced my raw breasts
and nuzzled my fingers, relics of her life
that even now to discard, to bury,
would somehow be to put that baby in the dirt:

In the dirt: where you are, somewhere,
if even that. Disposed of, the offal
of a rancid fear that I understand too well
and yet for you, my baby unborn,
unheld, scarcely even formed, I cannot
but resent its ascendancy over the compassion
that, in all other breaths, has been
your mother's signal trait. I run my thumb
across the little dents and fancy
I feel them pressing hard against your gums,
lancets of life ever dammed behind the flesh.

shadow-world

In the desert, the days are bleak with light,
heat that pounds with unrelenting ferocity
on earth whose stone has turned to sand
beneath the onslaught: I swept the light away,
dug out a quietude of shadow
beneath a stunted tree whose obstinacy
I claimed for your own, and there I laid
the relics of your name, hoping
that the shade of that austere canyon,
so hostile to the frailties of human flesh,
might for your unready and feckless feet
be refuge and playground,
that she, who scarcely mortal, never learned fear,
might practice some small humanity
among these rocks and thorns
before losing all hold on this carnal plane.

let's argue

I wonder if you grow frustrated
with your small space in my rooms,
only sized for an as-you-were,

if the sound of your name on my lips
grates you with its cloying phonation:

I like to think you push the walls,
break down the door,
dare me to yell at you,

get angry, get annoyed, get exasperated,
with you, find your growth unfamiliar
and your rebellion obnoxious:

I'm sorry I don't know how
to build bigger rooms for you,
sorry I only know the name
of the baby-that-wasn't, but I promise
if you call me out,
if you challenge me, defy me,
I will find a way to answer.

the snow makes me dream of deserts

I watch the snow rise in waves
and hurl itself at the glass, listen to the gale
as it bends all its strength along the earth,
and I am glad I anchored you
to a desert crag instead, glad your playground
has warm dust for your bare feet,

sun-split stones to scramble on,
stubborn scrub trees springing out of cliffs
to teach you whimsy and obstinance both:

I will sit in the frozen north
and think of you at play
with the other lost ones, so much older than you,
who built the cliff-clad homes
that I like to think you visit, when homesick
for a home that was so briefly yours,

and I am sure they made you one of their own,
that already you have far outpaced me,
that the baby I buried
has become as old and fulgid as the stars.

Coryphée

I Buried My Sparrow

They asked me to look in on her,
      to lay out the clothes for her going-away.
They wanted me to say, I see her,
      but I did not see her.
I could only see the owl, ugly night-bird,
      thief, spoiler, ravager, foe,
The devourer who had stolen her breath,
      under his silent wings and discarded
All her broken pieces here.

These shattered bones cannot hold her,
      they cannot frame her feral will.
This calm with which they have painted
      her face brings no calm to me –
It is my fierce child my fingers seek,
      my wanderer, my challenger, my coryphée:
I would pick out the feathers and piece
      back the wings death named dross,
But my little sparrow lies flightless still.

too late for that

perhaps she mothered too early,
like a flower that blooms
before the frost has done,
and in its brief, bright glory secures
its own undue end:
so she has finished with those colors –
having spent herself so fully and so soon,
she watches cold-eyed
as the petals brown and turn
and crumble to dust in a late winter wind.

star-catchers

glittering night succeeds lightless day
stars lie trapped under sheets of ice,
gazing heavenward where tracks of darkness
mark their former path, still spangled
with the ghostly trail of a forgotten glory:

the earth has laid siege to the sky,
capturing and holding hostage
in her snowy arms every orb and constellation
that might set fire to the night:

Let the gods and angels boast
the immortality of their tread –
we wandering frailties of dust will seize
on stars and find in our fists
flames to warm even the wintry grave.

Little Fire

changeling

it happened on the phone, so suddenly
and in the midst of so many other words:

how badly are you hurt
where are you
what about the other driver
can you breathe okay

that it wasn't until days later,
when I was alone,
that I was able to hear my son say

Good-bye, mom

I realized then, that, heedless with terror
and the blind need to fix this, must fix this,
I had gathered up this poor, other, broken boy,
born that night

full-grown and fully unready for this awful place,
his womb a mash-up of metal and glass,
car parts and broken limbs

gathered him into my arms and fought
to save him, to heal him, to help him,
and only later caught the echo
of my first son's final, fading farewell.

The Second Son

He walks between the inhalations,
darts past as my eyelids sweep up:

this corpse who wears my son's skin
and pleads with me from eyeless sockets:

He is the almost, the nearly,
the could-have-been and yet-to-come
of a night that spared his life
and took two others – he has nowhere
to go, this ghastly child who yet cannot
enter heaven but has lost his body here,
so I will carry him with me
and hope to keep him from his brother.

a wrecked accounting

I used to count your breaths,
crouched by your bed in the nursery half-light,
your thin t-shirt pulled up
so I could measure how tautly
the skin pulled across your ribs:
I measured those nights in minutes of air,
weighing in my unsure hands
a stone of life and a stone of death,
waiting on the instant when one less inhale
would tip the scale and so set in motion
another midnight emergency room trip:

and then came that night – that night –
the only *that night* in my new vocabulary –
when all the stones fell helter-skelter
and when the measure was made,
there were more deaths than could be matched up
to bodies, but the exhalations that pressed
against my ear, whose warmth fogged my palm,
attested to more living than whose form
could prove itself to the eye.
It is no great divide, after all, that separates
the dead and the living: only the weight of one breath.

counting dead chickens before they're hatched

I am weary of epitaphs,
insuperably tired of the sound –

//strike, scrape, strike
        the intimacy of violence, grain by grain,
reshaping, renaming stone//

the sound of that chisel marking out
a name, two dates, some stilted phrase
that only in its wanting manages to approach
the awfulness, the gaping, screaming emptiness
of its import: I lie awake,
counting days and ways rather than sheep,
jerked out of any half-hearted somnolence
by phantom phone calls, the echo
of his voice in my ear, and drearily I recount
to the night how I heard the news today,
the news that may yet come tomorrow,
or the tomorrow after that.

new definitions

beneath these scars that recall
so violent and horrific an event
are buried other scars, much more innocent
in their import: the fall you took
at the park when you were one
has on the cusp of manhood been buried
beneath the shrapnel of glass and steel
and energy, but regardless of their origin,
the interpretation of all scars is the same:

he healed.

for others, wounds are always wounds
till they are dust, but you are not they.
you have healed, you will be healed,
you will heal others.
reluctant badges, they nonetheless remain
proof of life, though that old proof,
of that former life, has forever vanished,
along with the boy who bore it.

no trades in this game

I keep them in my pockets –
the bits of auto glass I plucked
out of the dirt in that corner field:

less than an inch across, they still scarcely
hold their shape, as if the shattering
of that impact cannot be stilled
but must reverberate on and on and on:

at the grocery store, chatting with strangers,
or smiling at would-be friends
in the church foyer, walking on the beach
and *not walking into the sea*, I scrape my thumb
along their edges, in constant and pretended
imitation of the cuts ghosted on your face,
the cuts that did make ghosts of them two,
now my two, now our two –

I must keep this glass close,
trace the pattern of dirt that coats it
and think of all the blood lost in that dirt.

A mother oughtn't lose a son, and if she does,
it's best if she goes with him –
that's what they did, them two,
what we do, you and I.

I scrape my thumb across this glass,
and wish I could so easily steal your wounds
for my own, but I cannot.
So I scrape my thumb, and keep to the field.

an artist's price

the measure of your madness lies in the care
you take to leash it: you construct frame after frame,
filling each to its edges before breathlessly leaping
to the next, feeding your black dog as much beauty
as he will swallow – lines and equations,
light and exposure, order and order and order
and grace – I would calm his frothing appetite,
I would soothe his growls, but I know
how suddenly he will turn on us both
if his mouth is not filled: this pace may undo you,
the beast may begin to eat his own tail
and devour you too, but I do not know
how to temper the fury of his hunger.

Your frames, though – how beautiful they are.

scarecrow

I can't get off the field.

Such an ordinary place, hateful in its mundanity:
even the evidence of violence is paltry
compared to the force of its impact –
rutted earth and bits of glass that will seed
the earth with the fruit of death:

the cold, dry dirt has seeped into my marrow,
long fingers of dust circling my legs
and rooting me in this place
that uprooted, unrooted, all of you:

four thousand miles away, my tongue
is dry, my hands are dirty,
my heart is sealed up in three coffins,
and only two are buried.

The Sympathy of Goblins

I went to the Goblin-king
and offered all my poor sacrifices at his feet:
he did his best to grant my boon,
dressed me up in the costumes of the dead
and watched me play their wretched parts –
pity from a goblin doesn't come cheap,
they're not a sympathetic race by nature,
but his great gloomy eye turned gloomier still
and he raised a hand to halt my antics –

Even I, he told me, can't steal back
from death his bounty, and no enchantment
can redeem that one lost second
one second
whose dance you so gracelessly ape –
put your costumes aside,
there is no refuge from death in magic,
the accountant only tables his columns once.
Like me, you too can only meet your measure.

A Mother and Son

A Dread of Air

It sinks into my bones,
like a sack of stillborn kittens
sinks into the sea, a heavy, rolling weight

a horror of breathing

as if a surfeit of air might push back
the darkness that waits just beyond
the edge of this day: my chest
scarcely rises, my heart slaggishly sends
each solitary beat staggering after the next,
and my vision closes on small things:

the small clods of dirt, like pie crust dough
the small petals, brown and withered in the cold
the small hand-blocked letters,
spelling out names where stone will rest

the small graves in the horrible emptiness
of the prairie: I have a horror of breathing,
but this horror walks with me.
I cannot stop.

after the accident

doppelganger of my death, she dogs
my steps, tracing my intentions
with the fog of her stolen breath:
it is an illusion, this companionship,
a lie I tell myself
to mute the horror of her end
and my persistence, a way to make story
of an aborted line with no period.

someone's walking on my grave

the first time I met you,
you were a hand-written placard
standing crookedly in a pile of fresh-turned dirt

and I could see, from the one big mound
rather than two divided ones,
that they'd granted you the small mercy
of lying in the same grave as your son

but I didn't imagine
they'd let you share the one box
like I know you'd want to,
your arm around him so he wouldn't feel alone
in the cold and the dark

I know you'd want to,
'cause I'd want to,
and we're the same, you and me,
somehow occupying the same space
even though we wound up on opposite sides
of this mirror, staring at each other

through every glass: they won't let you
hold him now, so when I hold my son,
I'll hug him extra-tight for both of us.
there but for the –
graceless, there go I.
there go we all,
but not alone and not forgotten.

A New Companion

Almosts dwell in-between,
a place where absence is its own world,
where unspoken words are caught,
kept in pockets, scattered like birdseed
for the hungry: here,
they are all hungry.

Not the ravening appetite that drives
a hunt, but the hollow emptiness
that quietly gnaws on sinew and marrow:
You must be hungry too,
because you unroll my clenched fingers,
searching my palm, my pockets,
for crumbs of thought that taste
like what you remember of where you'd been,
when you were –

but I am empty of such gifts.
I did not know you back then,
and you will know no to-be,
so words of mine can offer no sustenance.
I cup your starving cheek,
lace your fingers in mine,
and keep your ache deep in my own belly.

Passengers

It's easier to pick up hitchhikers now
that I've grown so accustomed
to strangers in my car – in some ways,
maybe, it's a relief to have a passenger
who will tell me what sort of music
they like or where they're headed –

you and I will never be more than strangers,
never craft companionship of this alliance,
and though, consequent to intersection,
our roads cannot again diverge,
I'll never know

what you were saying
what music was playing
whether you ever saw the headlights:

Death has set us at odds, who were no enemies
and now cannot be friends,
but still I will keep this place for you,
I will say your name into the silence.

This is Kelly

one day I'll slip up
and introduce the ghost at my elbow
as if she were visible to all:
just another mother, like me,
of daughters and sons, another woman
driven from this need to that
till she was driven to the end
of all needs: the irony is,
you're not here at all.
your destination was far distant
from me, and no collision of mere steel
and glass and time could alter that.
No, I am haunted not by who you are
or even who you might have been,
but only by this brief impression,
this photograph of who you were
just then
just then
when all of our time each became the property
of the other, when death confettied our fates
and I seized a cold hand I cannot release.

outside looking in

I'm guessing you still see
the sunrises here from time to time,
even though you're out of time yourself:
as a mother, I doubt even eternity
possesses wonders sufficient to distract
you from your children for long – although
for you there is no long or short.

Even God himself kept an eye
on his offspring, his offshoot, his offering,
while the Lamb still wandered
these stony hills, so I suspect you, too,
must check in here, and I wonder
if your anger has abated,
if you still see my son as enemy to yours,
or if you have become the sum infinite
of all your finite addends,
if having learned in sheep's clothing
to mother a few, you now with the Lamb
look on our brief hours as mother to all.

the trees of winter

I look on winter with a jaundiced eye:
all her fairy castles, the worlds she builds
within a night, are too easily demolished –
it's not the cold sun that I resent,
the quiet drip-drip that heralds the slow remove
of beauty to sludge, of ice to the mundanity of mire:

no, it's the heedless step, the sudden jar,
the unanticipated brush of pine needles on my arm,
and with a whispered *hush*!
the whole tree is bereft of its treasured coat,
standing bare and plain and dark among its fancy fellows:

it reminds me of you, bright and glistening,
garbed in magic and promise and dazzling hope,
till one unsteady step shook it all loose,
and now only dark bones stand staunch in a world of
white.

Good Memoriam Copy

when Little Grandma died –
so named solely for her diminutive size
and not for any slightness of personality –
a preacher who'd never met her told lies
and made false promises over her casket:
as a child, I was glad of the excuse
to trade tears for anger –
I wept because she was dead,
because life had lost as it always did,
but his lies made me angrier than that truth:
she hadn't been nice or kind or loving
or even polite – her only softness
had been the slackness of her rotting skin
as she lay in the nursing home bed.
I was angry because it should have been enough
that she was gone, not that she'd been great.
I feel that childish stirring now, for you,
as I read the newspaper struggling
to make myth of your story:
an awkward, over-sized teenage boy barely laying hold
on who he would become just isn't good copy,
so you became a football hero, decked out with popularity
and uncommon kindness, and I am angry
for how little their well-dressed grief must resemble
the loss of your actual life – which is enough,
more than enough, for sorrow and for rage.

early days

I am waiting on a countersign,
but you refuse to offer me this kindness,
refuse any concession that might own us
allies; but for me, it is hard to find
an adversary any constant companion:

as I learn your quirks and foibles,
the uneven tenor of your voice,
the force and energy of your awkward limbs
that had almost made you a man
but still flounder and start like a boy,
I can only catalogue them with affection,

and hope that your steps will not diverge
from mine too soon, that you will give me leave
to carve out a memorial for here
before you quit me entirely.

Miscellany of Spirits

school shooting

I would gather up all your blood

it's wrong that it should lie there
like refuse, just wasted fluid
that needs scrubbing away

it carried life to your limbs, your head,
your heart: it was undone in its purpose
by a foul trick that turned its haste,
its diligence, into this travesty of effort:

it's not its fault that you lay there,
emptying out while a strange child
with a strange heart emptied his gun.
I've gathered up so many things
you heedlessly left behind –
your blanket, your bear, and later,
your keys, your phone, and always,
your underwear – I don't know how
to leave pieces of you strewn untended
now that you have run so far ahead:
I would gather all your blood.

Just One More (Omran Daqneesh)

He seemed a doll: a poor one,
his expression scarcely human,
his countenance a bleak pretend
at childishness – his pallor was unreal,
until I saw where tears had tracked
a brown path through the white ash,
where real red blood splashed its proof
on limbs too weak and wrecked
to tremble – even dolls are not so still.

Dolls bear the evidence of energy
in their pose, they tumble in remembrance
of their play, but this doll,

this boy
sits so still
transfixed by terrors no mind can hold

He holds himself. He waits.
He has no power, no comprehension,
no hope, no answer – even his brother,
blood of his blood, a heartbeat before his,
heart beats no more.

He waits.
How will we answer?
Call and repeat. Call and repeat.

The Empty Bowl

she lies on the ground
her fingers trace the stretch marks
that frame the golden bowl
of her belly – empty bowl
empty arms
but her eyes and ears are full
of a sea cold but not cruel:
cruelty denotes desire,
and she was robbed of all
she longed for by a beast
without hunger or want
only a mindless mouth –
these white lines are her only map
the only course of navigation
to a place called mother
she has no photos, no relics
of the beloved – once dear and familiar,
now only distant and sacred –
so she traces out the path on her skin,
remembers a weight, a warmth,
holds fast within herself
the memory of what bloomed there.

The Shoes By The Door (I'll Wait)

It's the nonchalance of the thing
that makes it impossible – just look
at your shoes tumbled there by the door.
You were in a hurry, I suppose,
perhaps distracted, and when one loafer
landed on top of your broken-down hiking boot,
you didn't bother to straighten it.
You needed new ones, anyway –

from here on the couch I can see
the worn imprint of your foot on the insole,
I can see the crease on the back
where you always shoved your foot in too quickly,
not pausing to unlace and relace,
I can see where the tongue is caught –

You'll need to pull that out
the next time you put them on.

The next time.

Even your shoes know this is ridiculous.
You can't just be gone as casually as that.
These things are supposed to happen
"in good time," but there was no order
to this. It doesn't make sense.
You need to come home and straighten your shoes.

The Sum of the Thing

lost contest

These spirit-cages God built
just don't last long: the locks rust out,
the bars bend, and often long before
the warden forgets his mandate,
the spirit breaks free.

Still, like foolish Arachne, I vaunt
my poor prowess against the divine,
hoping to imprison behind these bars of ink
some piece of your soul He has long set free.

That Which Persists

Strange that nothing is as ordinary
to this tenuous existence as to begin
and to end, and yet we find both
so remarkable, every time, as if
just discovering anew that life waits,
impatient, in bellies and eggs, and as impatiently
decamps for parts unknown, leaving scattered
smothered fires and abandoned purposes:

even animals mourn these commonplace departures,
as if they too, against all experience and reason,
imagined this day might be different
in its measure from every other: proof
of the divine, they say, lies in the very fact
of its conception, that in the face of invincible death,
we perceive indomitable life,
that though hobbled together with rusting joints
and decaying beams, we count our houses
impervious to rot and incapable of demolition:

something other than blood and bones
persuades even the beasts that breath ought not
to be extinguished, and so we all
linger when the frost falls, searching over and over again
for something familiar, some remnant that persists
outside of this seed case that has become unfamiliar
in its emptiness, our grief implacably at odds
with our conviction that all is not yet done,
that something more than just this broken machine,
designed for obsolescence, must continue.

small consolation

the reader, from whose hands your pages
were so abruptly snatched, has been cheated,
his heart hanging on a story whose end
he cannot conceive and whose parenthesis
he cannot suffer: he cannot accept
that only the medium of the tale has altered,
that the poor ink and paper
of blood and flesh have found their metamorphosis
in spirit and soul, that these invisible words
still carry your name and join your story
to a chronicle whose prologue and epilogue are the same.

why I will keep your dirty shoelaces

atheism is a poor prop to grief:
we are religious in our instincts,
making reliquary of outhouses if once
the lost relieved himself there:

a pair of underwear in the laundry basket,
an unwashed plate on a cluttered desk,
an impression on a pillow – all these take
a sacred shape and seem to carry some whisper
of the irreclaimable to our ears,
and we find ourselves desperate most to preserve
the most ephemeral proofs of their presence here.

scrimshaw

I collect bones like treasures,
the evidences of absence, and imagine
that on their frames I can hang
other, more paltry arts, as if in the embrace
of dread, dread takes on a kindness,
but there is nothing kind about nothing.

Talismans of my foolishness, these shards lie
scattered across notebooks and bookshelves,
marking out the boundaries of my own absence
and pretending to invite other wanderers in.

death's consort

spring calls in her chips:
torrents gush, transforming ice falls
to waterfalls and snowy fields to muddy pits:
bounty is confused with exorbitance
life soon becomes overripe
and all comers glut themselves on her fruits:
she is no less violent, no more reserved
or rational, than her counterpart,
as sudden and selfish in her demands.

The Long Walk

Hold my hand, darling,
it's dark out here
Chafe my hand, won't you,
it's cold out here
I can't feel your hand, darling,
please don't let go
I've lost my grip, dearest,
I'm so dark in here.

beachcomb

even on stony black shores like these,
where sullen waves shatter shells with abandon,
I am compelled to hunt for treasures,
behind rocks that may have shielded them
from the battery, or deep in the belly
of the ocean at low tide: my disquiet spirit
is quieted by the certitude of their spirals,
the doubtless impossibility of their perfect
and regular lines and angles, this preposterous insistence
that the Destroyer is still and always the Creator,
that savage and explosive violence can fashion
grace and order from bone and rock and wood.

the last marker

I've left this trail of stones for you –
I did learn from the fairytales, after all –
so you may find me wherever I am
in the earth and know that I keep bounded
a space yours alone, you who need
no space at all: you have maps and navigations
of which I know nothing, but I cannot leave
unmarked this journey, which though mine
in will is yours in debt, debt I refuse to discharge:
occupied or abandoned, this breach of being
with which I walk will always bear your name.

Acknowledgments

I would like to thank my husband, whose unflagging support through seemingly unending loss continues to be my point of navigation on starless nights.

This book would read very differently if not for the courage and compassion of first responders, and in particular, the firefighter who pulled my youngest from the wreckage on a dark, cold night.

My heart remains constant with Josh, Kelly, and Abigail, who walk with me on every trail.

Special consideration should be given to the tireless and creative efforts of the editing and design team of Cornerstone Press, who took my vision and made it their own, and hopefully, yours.

Every work of art is a collaboration between the artist and the one who experiences it, and so I thank you, the reader, for what you bring to this work and what you have made it.